ATMOSPHERE
AND WEATHER

ATMOSPHERE AND WEATHER

Terry Jennings

APR 1 8 2006

First published in 2005 by Evans Brothers Limited
2A Portman Mansions, Chiltern Street
London W1U 6NR

This edition published under license from Evans Brothers Limited.
All rights reserved.
Copyright © 2005 Evans Brothers Limited.

Designer: Giraffic Design, Editor: Mary-Jane Wilkins, Illustrator:
Graham Rosewarne, Series consultant: Steve Watts

Picture acknowledgements
Ecoscene: page 6, 7, 9 (top), 43 (middle), 44 (middle), 45
Terry Jennings: page 2, 4, 11, 12, 15, 16, 21, 22, 24, 36, 37,
39 (top), 43 (top)
Oxford Scientific: front cover, page 14, 19 (middle), 20, 23,
28, 32, 33, 34 (bottom), 35, 38, 41 (bottom), 44 (middle)
Science Photo Library: page 9, 15 (bottom), 31, 34 (top),
39 (bottom), 41 (top), 42

Published in the United States by Smart Apple Media
2140 Howard Drive West, North Mankato, Minnesota 56003

Library of Congress Cataloging-in-Publication Data

Jennings, Terry J.
Atmosphere and weather / by Terry Jennings.
p. cm. — (Weather and climate)
Includes index.
ISBN 1-58340-725-1
1. Troposphere—Juvenile literature. 2. Atmosphere—Juvenile
literature. 3. Weather—Juvenile literature. 4. Climatology—
Juvenile literature. I. Title.

QC881.2.T75J46 2005
551.6—dc22   2004065308

9 8 7 6 5 4 3 2 1

Contents

The importance of weather

People have always been interested in the weather because of its huge effect on our lives. The weather determines not only the type of houses we live in, but also the clothes we wear when we go out and whether or not we can play our favorite sport.

Ships' captains, fishermen, airline pilots, and motorists need to know about weather conditions so that they can travel safely. The weather also affects the types of plants and animals that share our part of Earth, the foods we eat, and the farming methods used to produce that food. Farmers, perhaps more than anyone else, are at the mercy of the weather because an unexpected frost, hailstorm, or drought can destroy a tender crop, while too much rain can cause destructive floods.

The sun's heat powers all of our weather. The weather in the middle latitudes is so changeable that many vacationers travel long distances to spend time in warm sunshine, such as here in Benidorm, Spain.

Drought can devastate tender crops. This field of sweet corn was destroyed by the drought that affected large parts of the United Kingdom in 1995.

What is weather?

Weather is the condition of the air at a certain time or over a brief period of time. Weather includes the temperature, the air pressure, the strength and direction of the wind, visibility, how much moisture the air contains, the cloud cover, and the amount and type of precipitation. These and other factors combine to give us fine, sunny days or cold, wet ones. The study of weather is called meteorology. Meteorologists study the atmosphere—the thin layer of air around Earth—and the causes of weather. Some meteorologists work at weather stations, collecting information about atmospheric movements of all kinds, while others work at forecasting centers.

Weather and climate

Climate differs from weather, because climate is the average, or usual, weather of a place over a long period of time. Climatologists study Earth's climates and how they affect plants, animals, and people. They are interested in past and present climatic changes. They also investigate how human activities affect world climates.

Air and atmosphere

The atmosphere is a thin layer of air surrounding Earth. Air itself is a mixture of gases—roughly four-fifths nitrogen and one-fifth oxygen, with traces of carbon dioxide, argon, and other gases such as xenon, neon, and krypton. There is also water in the atmosphere in the form of the invisible gas water vapor and as tiny water droplets and ice crystals in clouds.

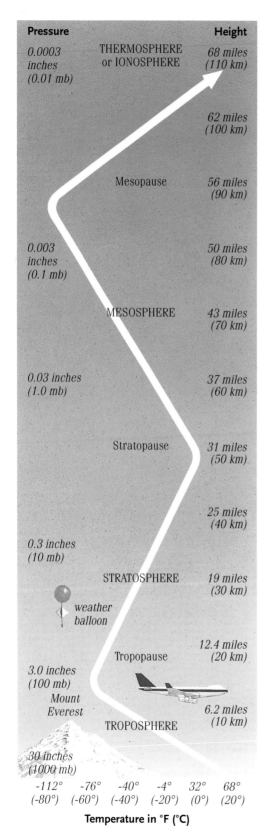

Pressure		Height
0.0003 inches (0.01 mb)	THERMOSPHERE or IONOSPHERE	68 miles (110 km)
		62 miles (100 km)
	Mesopause	56 miles (90 km)
0.003 inches (0.1 mb)		50 miles (80 km)
	MESOSPHERE	43 miles (70 km)
0.03 inches (1.0 mb)		37 miles (60 km)
	Stratopause	31 miles (50 km)
		25 miles (40 km)
0.3 inches (10 mb)		
	STRATOSPHERE	19 miles (30 km)
	weather balloon	
	Tropopause	12.4 miles (20 km)
3.0 inches (100 mb)		
Mount Everest		6.2 miles (10 km)
	TROPOSPHERE	
30 inches (1000 mb)		

-112° (-80°) -76° (-60°) -40° (-40°) -4° (-20°) 32° (0°) 68° (20°)

Temperature in °F (°C)

Atmospheric layers

The atmosphere is between 100 and 200 miles (160 and 320 km) thick and is made up of several layers. These extend from Earth and fade out into space. All of our weather occurs in the layer of the atmosphere nearest Earth's surface. This layer, called the troposphere, extends up to about 5 miles (8 km) near the poles and 10 miles (16 km) near the equator. The troposphere contains 80 percent of all the gases in the atmosphere. The temperature decreases with height in the troposphere. This is because the atmosphere does not receive its heat directly from the sun, but indirectly from the surface of Earth.

The layer above the troposphere is called the stratosphere. This layer, which extends up to about 30 miles (50 km), contains about 19 percent of all the gases in the atmosphere. In the stratosphere, the temperature is higher because it contains the ozone layer. The ozone layer absorbs most of the sun's harmful ultraviolet radiation, preventing it from reaching Earth. Long-distance jet aircraft fly in the stratosphere at heights of about 33,000 feet (10,000 m), where they are above the weather, and the air is still.

In the topmost layer of the atmosphere, the exosphere, there are almost no gases, and here the atmosphere merges into space.

Air pressure

Air has weight, and it presses on things in all directions with a force called air pressure, or atmospheric pressure. Over 10 square feet (1 sq m), the weight of air pressing down is heavier than a large elephant. Air pressure is greatest near the ground and decreases with height. At 33,000 feet (10,000 m) above the ground, where jet aircraft fly, the air pressure is very low, and the weight of air pressing down on the aircraft is less. Because there is less air and oxygen, aircraft cabins have to be pressurized so that the passengers and crew can breathe. The air pressure inside the aircraft is roughly the same as at ground level.

Earth's atmosphere is made up of several layers. All of our weather occurs within the lowest layer, the troposphere.

Depressions and anticyclones

Air pressure plays an important part in creating different weather conditions, especially winds. Low atmospheric pressure areas, or depressions, cause unsettled weather in parts of the United States, Britain, Europe, and many other locations in the middle latitudes. The other main air system in these latitudes is an anticyclone. This is an area of high pressure. Anticyclones are associated with settled weather. In the summer, there may be a succession of hot, sunny days. But in the winter, anticyclones may bring cold weather and fog.

Measuring air pressure

Air pressure is measured with a barometer. The first barometers were made from a long, vertical tube, closed at the top and opening at the bottom into a dish. Both the dish and the tube contained mercury. There was no air above the column of mercury; instead, there was an empty space, or vacuum. As the air pressure increased, it pushed down on the mercury in the dish, forcing it up the tube, where its height was measured against a scale. When the air pressure fell, the height of the mercury also fell. Air pressure is measured in millibars or inches. The average pressure at sea level is 20 inches (1013.25 mb).

A barometer measures the air pressure. This barometer, called a barograph, records the air pressure automatically on a revolving drum.

More portable than a mercury barometer, and easier to use, is an aneroid barometer. This has a needle and dial above a sealed metal box containing a partial vacuum. When air presses against the metal box, a series of springs and levers move the needle. The greater the air pressure, the farther the needle moves in a clockwise direction. The lower the air pressure, the farther the needle moves counterclockwise.

THE FIRST BAROMETER

Italian Evangelista Torricelli made the first barometer in 1644. He filled a three-foot-long (1 m) glass tube with mercury and held the open end under the surface of a bowl of mercury. The level of the mercury in the tube dropped to about 32 inches (80 cm), leaving a vacuum at the top. Torricelli realized that the weight, or pressure, of the air on the mercury in the bowl held up the column of mercury in the tube. French mathematician Blaise Pascal was interested in Torricelli's work. In 1648, Pascal proved that the atmosphere has weight (or pressure) by sending his brother-in-law up a mountain with a barometer. The level of mercury in the barometer tube dropped more the higher he climbed.

The power of the sun

2

The weather on Earth varies enormously from place to place at any particular moment. Different places have sunshine, sweltering heat, thick clouds, freezing conditions, blinding snow, howling gales, or torrential rain. The sun powers all of these changes in the weather.

Heat from the sun

Temperature is the most important factor affecting the weather. It is controlled by the sun. Temperature is a measure of heat or cold, and the amount of heat that reaches Earth's surface varies from place to place. Generally, the sun's heat is greatest around the equator and decreases toward the poles.

The atmosphere absorbs some of the sun's heat, and because Earth's surface is curved, the sun's rays have to pass through a thicker atmosphere near the poles. As a result, less heat reaches the ground near the poles, so they are much cooler than the areas near the equator. The sun's rays are also spread over a larger area near the poles, again because of the curvature of Earth's surface, so they have less warming power.

**THE EFFECT OF EARTH'S CURVATURE
ON THE SUN'S RAYS**

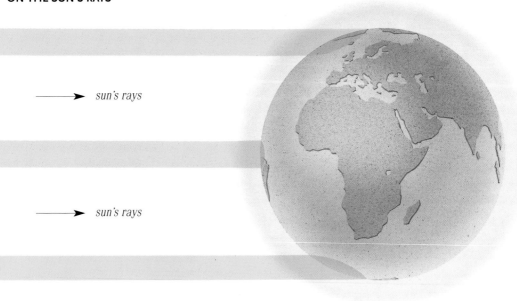

sun's rays

sun's rays

Seasonal changes

There are seasonal differences in temperature in many parts of the world. As Earth orbits the sun, its axis is tilted by 23.5°, which means that the amount of heat received at most places varies according to the time of year. This causes the seasons.

On March 21, the sun is above the equator. The sun's rays are spread evenly over Earth, and all places have equal day and night. This is the vernal (or spring) equinox in the northern hemisphere and the autumn equinox in the southern hemisphere.

On December 21, Earth's southern hemisphere is tilted toward the sun, which is above the Tropic of Capricorn. This is the winter solstice (the shortest day) in the northern hemisphere and the summer solstice (the longest day) in the southern hemisphere.

March 21

June 21

Sun

December 21

September 22

On June 21, the northern hemisphere is tilted toward the sun. The sun is above the Tropic of Cancer. This is the summer solstice in the northern hemisphere and the winter solstice in the southern hemisphere.

On September 22, the sun is again above the equator. This is the autumn equinox in the northern hemisphere and the vernal, or spring, equinox in the southern hemisphere. Again, day and night are equal length.

In temperate climates, the four seasons are marked by changes to deciduous trees, as shown by this oak tree, photographed in spring, summer, autumn, and winter.

Temperature variations

Temperatures on Earth vary from place to place because of latitude and altitude. Temperatures are much higher near the equator than near the poles. Over Earth as a whole, the temperature drops gradually as you move north or south away from the equator. This is described as a gradual reduction of temperature with increasing latitude.

The sun does not warm the air directly. It warms Earth, which heats the air above it. As a result, the higher you go above Earth the less the air is warmed. If you climb a mountain, there is a noticeable drop in temperature as you move away from the source of heat. On average, the temperature falls 3.5 °F (2 °C) for every 1,000 feet (300 m) you climb. This reduction in temperature with altitude has several effects. Quito, the capital of Ecuador, lies almost on the equator in South America. But its average temperature is only 55 °F (13 °C) because it lies in a narrow valley in the Andes Mountains, 9,250 feet (2,820 m) above sea level.

Plant life is also affected by changes of temperature with altitude. Deciduous forests grow below 2,500 feet (760 m) on Mount Washington in New Hampshire. Above 2,500 feet (760 m) is mixed forest, which merges into coniferous forest at 3,200 feet (980 m). Between 4,000 and 5,000 feet (1,220–1,520 m), small shrubs grow. The height above which trees will not grow is called the timberline. The tops of the highest mountains, even near the equator, are always snowy. The snow line is the line above which snow does not melt in summer.

The height above which trees cannot grow on a mountain is called the timberline. The tops of the highest mountains, such as these in the Austrian Alps, are permanently covered with snow.

The effect of land and sea

The nearness of an ocean or sea has a big effect on temperature. When the sun's heat strikes land, only a very thin layer of soil and rock absorbs the heat. So the land warms up fast but also loses heat fast. Over the oceans, the sun's heat penetrates deeply and warms a greater volume. The oceans warm up slowly but hold their heat much longer.

Places near oceans and seas have a much smaller difference in temperature between summer and winter than places far inland. Edinburgh and Moscow are both about the same distance from the equator. The average maximum temperature in Edinburgh is 43 °F (6 °C) in January and 64 °F (18 °C) in July. By contrast, the average maximum in Moscow is 16 °F (–9 °C) in January and 73 °F (23 °C) in July. Moscow is far from the sea, so summers there can be very hot, and winters are severe. Edinburgh is close to the sea and has no extremes of temperature.

Cloud barriers

Clouds act as barriers to the sun's rays. So the world's highest temperatures are recorded not in the cloudy regions near the equator, but under the clear, sunny skies of hot deserts farther north or south. Clouds also reduce the loss of heat from the land, so cloudy regions have a small daily range of temperature, compared with the hot days and cold nights of the deserts. In Europe and North America, the lowest temperatures are recorded on winter nights when there are clear, starlit skies and no clouds to reduce the loss of heat from the land.

Ocean currents

The waters of the oceans mix and circulate. Warm water from the tropics flows toward the poles, while cold water from the polar regions flows toward the equator. Sometimes currents form a stream, such as the Gulf Stream. Most currents are caused by winds that blow in the same direction all the time.

The main ocean currents in the North Atlantic. Cold currents are shown in blue and warm currents in red.

The Gulf Stream begins with warm (79 to 84 °F [26–29 °C]) water near the equator in the Gulf of Mexico. This flows up the east coast of the U.S., warming the land. The Gulf Stream then flows across the Atlantic Ocean and fans out into the North Atlantic Drift. The warm air over them brings milder winters to parts of northwest Europe than might be expected for places so far north.

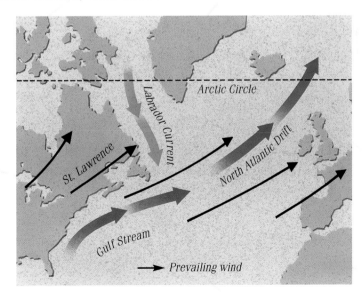

Labrador Current

Arctic Circle

St. Lawrence

North Atlantic Drift

Gulf Stream

Prevailing wind

Huge waves on the coast of Southern California caused by an El Niño event in February 1998.

Warm winds

The winds that blow over warm ocean currents to the land are warmed by the currents. These winds carry moisture and often bring rain. Winds that blow over cold currents, such as the Labrador Current, which flows south from the Arctic between Greenland and eastern Canada, are cool. They do not hold much moisture, so they dry the land.

The effect of an ocean on the temperature is reduced as you travel away from it. The prevailing winds in the British Isles come from the southwest. They are formed over the Atlantic Ocean and warmed by the Gulf Stream and the North Atlantic Drift. They are relatively warm in the winter and cool in the summer, and produce similar temperatures over the British Isles. The prevailing winds on the eastern coast of the U.S. also come from the southwest, but they blow over the North American continent. So the eastern coast of the U.S. has hot summers, cold winters, and a wide annual range of temperatures.

The effect of relief

Earth's shape (its relief) also creates temperature differences. Vineyards and orchards are planted on the sides of valleys, rather than in the fertile soil in the bottom of the valleys. This is because heavy, cold air moves down the slopes and collects in valley bottoms. For similar reasons, Alpine villages are built on the north sides of valleys that run from east to west. This way, they receive more of the sun's warmth. Mountains also provide shelter from cold winds.

The village of Rickmansworth, northwest of London, is in a frost hollow where cold air collects in the bottom of a valley. Here, temperatures can be 27 °F (15 °C) lower than in central London, only 15 miles (24 km) away.

Measuring temperature

Air temperature is measured with a dry-bulb thermometer. This narrow, sealed tube of glass has a bulb at one end. The mercury inside expands and contracts with changes in the air temperature.

Meteorologists record the highest and lowest temperature over every 24 hours with two special thermometers. The maximum thermometer records the highest temperature. It is like a dry-bulb thermometer, except that the glass tube narrows near the bulb. As the temperature rises, the mercury expands. When the temperature falls, the mercury contracts, but the narrow tube prevents it from going back into the bulb. The top of the mercury column shows the highest temperature.

The minimum thermometer measures the lowest temperature. It is filled with alcohol and has a small pin inside. This is carried toward the bulb as the temperature falls and the alcohol contracts. When the temperature rises again, the alcohol expands, and the pin is left in the tube. The end of the pin farthest from the bulb marks the minimum temperature. These thermometers are mounted horizontally so that gravity does not affect the readings. Both are reset every day. A double-ended thermometer can also measure these temperatures. It contains mercury and has a small pin in each tube to record the maximum and minimum temperature.

HOT AND COLD

The hottest place on Earth is El Azizia in the Libyan desert. On September 13, 1922, a temperature of 136.4 °F (58 °C) was recorded. The world's lowest temperature, −128.5 °F (−89.2 °C), was recorded at Vostok Scientific Station, Antarctica, on July 21, 1983.

The small pins in this double-ended maximum and minimum thermometer are reset by a push-button mechanism.

Sunshine recorders

Most seaside cities record the sunshine they receive daily, often using a Campbell-Stokes sunshine recorder. Every day, a light-sensitive card is fitted into the semicircular frame. When the sun shines, the glass ball mounted in front of the card focuses the sun's rays so that a mark is burned on the card. As Earth turns, the burn mark moves along the card. No marks are made when the sun is not shining. The card is marked in hours and parts of hours, which makes it easy to add up the length of time the sun shone on any day.

The sun's rays pass through the glass sphere of a Campbell-Stokes sunshine recorder in the Hoggar Mountains of Algeria.

Wind

3

Wind is moving air. Earth's atmosphere is always moving, and currents of air move from place to place as wind. We cannot see the wind, but we can feel it. We can also see the effects of wind—for example, when it rustles the leaves of trees, makes branches sway, or makes waves crash on the seashore.

Strong winds have pruned this hedge near the east coast of Norfolk, England, so that it is bent over in the direction of the prevailing wind.

Strong winds that nearly always blow from the same direction are called prevailing winds. In exposed areas, you can tell the direction from which the prevailing wind blows. It prevents trees from growing upright, so they are bent over in the direction the wind blows.

Why do winds blow?

Winds blow from place to place because the sun warms some parts of Earth more than others. Air over warmer ground is also warmed. As the air increases in temperature, it expands and becomes less dense, or "lighter." Because it is "lighter" than the surrounding air, the warm air rises in the same way that a hot-air balloon rises.

The rising warm air is replaced by cooler air moving in from the surrounding area. This creates winds close to the ground. When the rising warm air reaches the upper atmosphere, it rushes to replace the sinking cooler air, creating upper-level winds and completing the cycle.

Land and sea breezes

To understand how and why winds blow, think of a gentle wind, or breeze, near the coast. On a sunny morning by the coast, the land heats up faster than the sea, and it warms the air above it. The warmer air expands and begins to rise. This lowers the air pressure above the land, so cooler air is drawn in from the sea as a sea breeze.

Meanwhile, over the sea, the air is still cool and sinking. This increases the air pressure over the sea. High in the sky, winds fed by the air rising over the land blow out to sea to replace the sinking air. During the late evening of the same day, the direction of the winds is

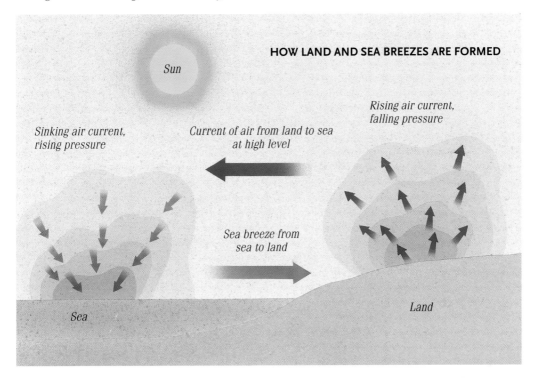

HOW LAND AND SEA BREEZES ARE FORMED

Sun

Rising air current, falling pressure

Sinking air current, rising pressure

Current of air from land to sea at high level

Sea breeze from sea to land

Sea

Land

reversed. This is because the sea keeps its warmth longer than the land. Air flowing away from the seashore is called a land breeze.

World winds

To the north of the equator lies the Tropic of Cancer and, an equal distance south, lies the Tropic of Capricorn. The region between the two, known as the tropics, receives far more heat from the sun than the areas outside it receive.

As the land near the equator is heated, the hot air above it rises. Because hot air is "lighter," or less dense, than cold air, the air pressure around the equator is low. The hot air cools as it rises and eventually flows to the north and south. It sinks back to Earth in the zones of high pressure about 30° north and south. These belts of calm or light winds are sometimes called the horse latitudes, although no one is sure where the name came from.

From the horse latitudes, winds called trade winds blow back toward the doldrums, or the belt of calm air with high humidity and high temperatures near the equator, while westerly winds blow toward the poles.

Above Earth's poles, with their vast areas of ice and snow, the air is cooled. It sinks and spreads outward. These cold winds are called polar easterlies, and when they reach Earth's middle latitudes (midway between the equator and the poles), they meet warmer winds. The boundary where this happens is called the polar front. As the two sets of winds collide, they do not mix but instead produce frontal depressions (see page 30).

Prevailing winds

Trade winds, westerlies, and polar easterlies are the world's prevailing winds. These winds do not blow in straight north-south lines. This is because Earth spins on its axis, and this spin produces the Coriolis effect, which throws winds sideways from their path. In the northern hemisphere, winds are thrown to the right of their path, so the trade winds north of the equator blow from the northeast to the southwest. In the southern hemisphere, the winds curve to the left.

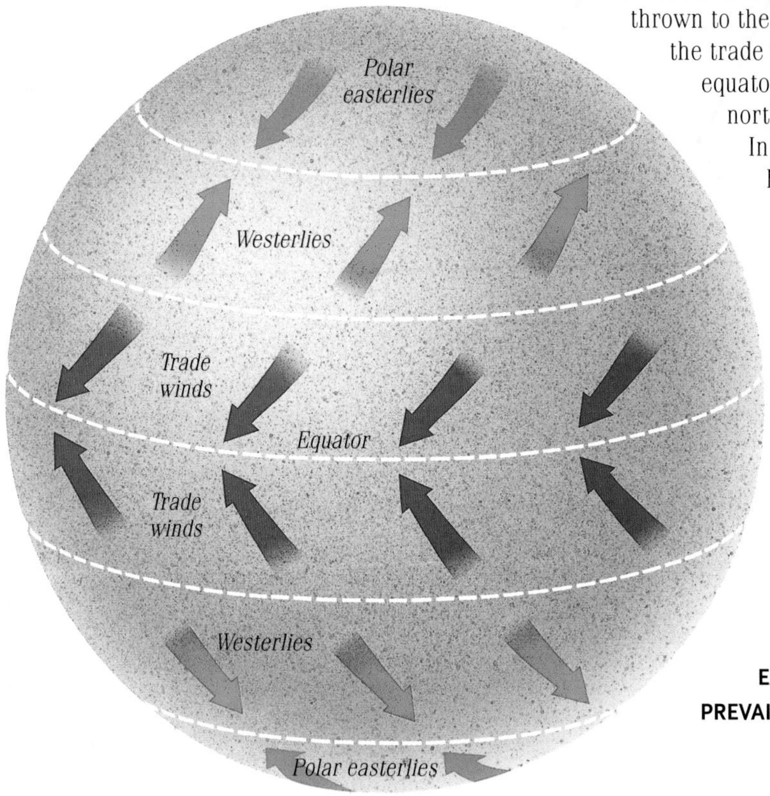

Polar easterlies

Westerlies

Trade winds

Equator

Trade winds

Westerlies

Polar easterlies

EARTH'S PREVAILING WINDS

Other factors, such as mountain ranges and valleys, or friction with the land, also affect winds. In high and low pressure air systems (anticyclones and depressions), winds spiral around the center, like bath water around an open drain.

Monsoon winds change direction according to the season. In the summer, these winds carry moisture evaporated from the sea. This moisture falls as rain on land areas in southern Asia. In the winter, the direction of the winds is reversed, and dry winds blow away from the land toward the sea. Like sea breezes, monsoon winds are the result of unequal heating of land and sea. In the summer, the land area of southern Asia heats up rapidly, and low pressure results. Warm, moist winds sweep in from the sea as the summer monsoon. In the winter, the land areas of southern Asia lose heat rapidly. The low temperatures lead to very high pressure, and cold, dry air moves away from the land toward the relatively warm air and low pressure over the sea.

Flooding caused by heavy rain during the summer monsoon season in Vietnam.

Hurricanes

You can see the full power of moving air in the violent storms we call hurricanes and tornadoes. Hurricanes begin over the warm waters of the Atlantic Ocean, where the temperature is higher than 80 °F (27 °C). Meteorologists believe that hurricanes form when the air is warmer than the surface of the ocean. The storms pick up vast amounts of energy and moisture as they rush toward the land.

Hurricanes are among the most ferocious of windstorms and cause widespread damage. This damage was caused by Hurricane Andrew when it hit Florida in August 1992.

A hurricane can measure 250 miles (400 km) across. Inside of it, swirling winds spiral upward. At the center, or eye, of a hurricane, the skies are clear. The calm eye may be 25 miles (40 km) across, but the strongest winds, with speeds of up to 220 miles (350 km) per hour, are immediately around it. Hurricanes often travel over the Caribbean Islands and North America. High winds and torrential rains can cause massive damage to crops and property, and they sometimes also kill people. These kinds of storms are known as typhoons in the China Sea, cyclones in the Bay of Bengal, and willy-willies off the northwest coast of Australia.

HURRICANE NAMES

When a hurricane is first spotted, meteorologists give it a name to identify it. The first hurricane of the season is given a name beginning with the letter "A," the next "B," and so on. This custom was first started by Australian weather forecaster Clement Wragge (1852–1922), who used names from the Bible. Since 1978, meteorologists have drawn up a list of alternate male and female names in alphabetical order. Each new hurricane is given the next name on the list.

TORNADO ZONES

Some places have frequent tornadoes. The stretch of land that runs from the Gulf of Mexico through the states of Texas, Oklahoma, Kansas, Nebraska, and the Dakotas has so many tornadoes that it is known as "tornado alley." It has about 700 tornadoes every year. They are caused by cold, dry air masses from Canada meeting warm, wet air from the Gulf of Mexico.

In a violent tornado, the wind can reach speeds of more than 500 miles (800 km) per hour. This brings massive destruction and can leave hundreds of people injured and homeless. This is the devastation left by a tornado that struck Saragosa, Texas, in May 1997.

Tornadoes

Tornadoes are small, extremely powerful whirlwinds that form very suddenly. Every tornado is a violent, rapidly twisting funnel of cloud that stretches from a storm cloud to the ground. In the U.S., where tornadoes are common, they are often called twisters. Tornadoes can be as small as a few feet or as big as 330 feet (100 m) across, and they travel over the land at speeds of 18 to 40 miles (30–65 km) per hour. But inside a tornado are the highest wind speeds on Earth. These speeds can reach more than 500 miles (800 km) per hour.

A tornado destroys everything in its path, which can extend for more than 125 miles (200 km), before it uses up all of its energy. On average, there are about 1,000 tornadoes in the U.S. every year, and they also happen regularly in parts of Canada, Argentina, China, Australia, southwest Asia, and even Europe. In Britain, there are between 15 and 30 tornadoes a year.

A tornado that forms over a lake or the sea is called a waterspout.

RAINING FROGS

From time to time, people report seeing frogs, fish, and other small animals falling from the sky during rainstorms. These animals were probably sucked up from ponds and rivers by small tornadoes and then fell to the ground again with the rain.

THE BEAUFORT SCALE

We can estimate wind speed using the Beaufort
Scale. This was developed in 1805 by Sir Francis
Beaufort to estimate wind speed at sea. It was
later extended to include exact wind speeds and
adapted for use on land.

Beaufort number	Miles per hour (km per hour)	Wind description
0	Less than 1	Calm
1	1–3 (1.6–5)	Light air movement
2	4–7 (6–11)	Slight breeze
3	8–12 (12–19)	Gentle breeze
4	13–18 (20–28)	Moderate breeze
5	19–24 (29–38)	Fresh breeze
6	25–31 (39–49)	Strong breeze
7	32–38 (50–61)	Moderate gale (or high wind)
8	39–46 (62–74)	Gale
9	47–54 (75–88)	Strong gale
10	55–63 (89–102)	Storm
11	64–72 (103–117)	Violent storm
12	73+ (118+)	Hurricane

Measuring wind speed and direction

Wind direction is shown by a wind vane or
weather vane. This is an arrow that turns on
a pivot. The tail of the arrow is larger than its
head. When the wind strikes the tail, it turns
the arrow to point in the direction from which
the air is coming. This is used as the name of
the wind, so that a westerly wind blows from
the west. At airfields, a windsock is used not
only to show wind direction but also to give an
indication of wind speed. The more horizontal
the sock is, the stronger the wind.

An anemometer gives an accurate
measurement of wind speed. This instrument is
usually mounted 33 feet (10 m) up a pole or on
a building, although handheld versions are
available. Three or four cups are attached to a
spindle. As the wind blows the cups around,
the spindle turns; the greater the wind force,
the faster the cups turn. The spindle is
attached to a device for measuring the wind
speed. Usually this is a dial like a car
speedometer.

*The cup anemometer, invented in 1846,
measures and records wind speeds.*

Water in the air

4

The atmosphere always contains the invisible gas water vapor. Most of this water vapor is in the troposphere, the lowest layer of the atmosphere. Water vapor is continuously formed as the sun warms oceans, seas, lakes, rivers, and other wet surfaces, and as water evaporates from plants.

Relative humidity
The temperature of the air determines how much water vapor it can hold. Warm air holds more water vapor than cold air. As a result, the air over hot deserts often contains much more water vapor than the air over cooler lands. But the water vapor in the hot air rarely condenses into visible water droplets because the air has to cool below the dew point before condensation occurs. The dew point is the temperature at which the air is saturated—that is, when the air contains all the water vapor that it can hold at that temperature. Meteorologists say that the air at dew point has a relative humidity of 100 percent. The relative humidity is the ratio between the amount of water vapor in the air and the maximum amount that it can hold at that temperature.

Condensation
For water vapor in the air to become liquid water, it must be cooled so that it condenses. Sometimes, when the sun comes out after a summer shower, you see steam rising from a road. The sun's heat turns water on the blacktop into water vapor. The colder air above the blacktop turns the water vapor back into the small water droplets we see as steam.

Below the dew point, water vapor in the atmosphere condenses around tiny bits of dust, plant pollen, or salt from the oceans to form droplets of water or tiny ice crystals. The droplets of water and ice crystals are so small that they remain suspended in the air. Masses of these particles form clouds in the air, and fog, mist, and dew near the ground.

WET ATMOSPHERE
Scientists estimate that at any one time the atmosphere contains about 4,070 trillion gallons (15,470 trillion l) of water. Because of the pull of Earth's gravity, nearly all of this water is in the troposphere, the layer of the atmosphere closest to Earth's surface.

Advection fog (see page 23) in the Austrian Alps. Cool, dense air rolled down into the valley during the night, and its moisture condensed into this blanket of fog.

Fog and mist

Fog and mist are clouds at ground level. They form in calm, clear weather. The most common kind of fog forms at night when the land in low-lying areas cools enough to bring the air above to its dew point. Water vapor in the cooling air condenses into water droplets. They are so light that they remain suspended in the air. The fog spreads slowly up from the ground and is called radiation fog. Radiation fog causes many aircraft and car accidents.

The other kind of fog, called advection fog, forms where a warm, moist wind blows over a cooler surface. Advection fog often forms in the harbor in San Francisco because warm, moist air from the south blows over cool ocean currents flowing down from the Arctic. Advection fog also forms in valleys. There, air that has cooled and become denser during the night rolls down into a valley from the surrounding hills or mountains. Condensation then occurs, and the valley fills with fog.

In mist, we can see more than 3,300 feet (1,000 m) but less than 6,600 feet (2,000 m). Fogs are thicker. In fog, the visibility is less than 3,300 feet (1,000 m), and it may drop to only 3 feet (1 m) or so. Mist and fog formed by radiation usually clear quickly when the temperature rises. Advection fogs are slow to clear because they disperse only when there is a change in the conditions that caused them.

Dew drops

Dew is drops of water deposited on blades of grass, cobwebs, stones, and other objects. Dew is formed under the same conditions as mist and fog, except that the air is still. Only the lowest layer of the atmosphere is cooled. As the temperature of this layer falls below the dew point, the water vapor in the air condenses, and drops of water are deposited on the ground. You can see similar condensation on the outside of an ice-cold glass of water. Dew often forms on grasses and other plants because their leaves give out moisture. As a result, the air next to the leaves has a high humidity, and little cooling is needed to make the water vapor condense.

Dew is a thin coating of water droplets that condenses on spiders' webs, grass, stones, and other surfaces when the air is cooled to below the dew point.

On calm winter nights, air that touches the ground may be chilled so that the water vapor in it turns into ice crystals. The resulting layer of frost may be so thick that it looks like snow, as on the fruit and leaves of this ivy plant.

How frost is formed

Frost, like fog, forms on clear nights when there are no clouds to reduce heat loss from Earth. For frost to form, the temperature must drop to below the freezing point, which is 32 °F (0 °C). True frost, or hoar frost, is formed when a thin layer of moist air near the ground cools quickly to below freezing. The water vapor in the air forms ice crystals, without condensing to liquid water, or dew. The crystals coat any cold surface.

The water cycle

The water in the atmosphere and the processes of evaporation and condensation are vital parts of the water cycle. Land plants and animals need a regular supply of fresh water, and this is produced by

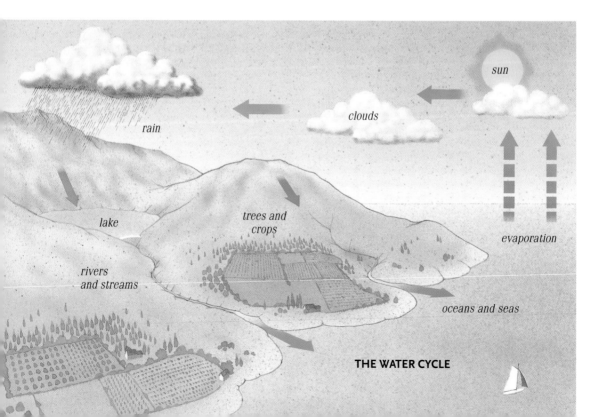

sun

clouds

rain

evaporation

lake

trees and crops

rivers and streams

oceans and seas

THE WATER CYCLE

the water cycle. The oceans and seas contain about 97 percent of the world's water, and scientists believe that nearly 90 percent of the water in the atmosphere comes from the oceans. The rest comes from seas, lakes, rivers, ponds, plants, and other moist surfaces. Over the oceans, the sun's rays evaporate water, which becomes water vapor. Rising air currents carry it upward. As it rises, it gradually cools. When it has cooled below the dew point, the water vapor condenses into tiny droplets of water or minute crystals of ice that form clouds.

Winds blow the clouds toward the land. When they are forced to rise over mountains, they are cooled further. They grow larger until the moisture in them falls as rain, snow, sleet, or hail.

The main precipitation in temperate regions is rain. Some of the rain sinks into the soil and is taken up by the roots of plants. Most of this water evaporates from the plant leaves and returns to the air. Some water sinks through the soil into the rocks below. This water may return to the surface as springs, the sources of rivers, which carry water back to the sea, completing the water cycle.

In high mountain and polar regions, precipitation is mainly snow. The snow piles up and is compressed into ice. Large bodies of ice, ranging from huge ice sheets to glaciers, flow downhill toward the sea. On the coast, icebergs break off from the ice sheets and glaciers. When the icebergs melt in the sea, they complete the water cycle in another way.

Measuring humidity

Meteorologists measure relative humidity with two identical thermometers. One, the dry-bulb thermometer, measures the air temperature. The other, the wet-bulb thermometer, has a piece of wet muslin wrapped around its bulb and dipped in water. The lower the humidity of the air, the more water evaporates from the muslin. Evaporating water is cooling. You feel this when sweat evaporates from your skin after vigorous exercise, and you start to shiver. Evaporation lowers the temperature of the wet-bulb thermometer. The relative humidity is the difference in temperature between the thermometers.

If the wet- and dry-bulb readings are the same, the air is saturated and has a relative humidity of 100 percent.

Absolute humidity measures the amount of water vapor in a given volume of air. The amount of water vapor the air can hold increases with temperature, so relative humidity is a more useful measurement.

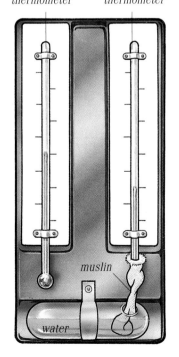

dry-bulb thermometer   *wet-bulb thermometer*

muslin

water

WET- AND DRY-BULB THERMOMETERS

The relative humidity is calculated from the difference in the temperatures shown by these wet- and dry-bulb thermometers.

Clouds

Clouds form when air is
cooled until the water vapor
condenses into water droplets.
These droplets are so small that they
remain suspended in the air, forming
a cloud. If it is very cold, the vapor
freezes into clouds of tiny ice crystals.

All clouds are in the troposphere, usually up to about 10 miles
(16 km). Here the temperature drops with height, so when
moist air rises, it cools, and clouds form. The temperature at
the top of the troposphere is well below freezing, at about
−67 °F (−55 °C). If the atmosphere were completely clean, no
clouds would form because there would be nothing for the water
vapor to condense on. But the air is laden with minute floating
particles such as dust, soot, salt from the sea, and plant pollen.
These allow water vapor in the air to condense. Near the
ground, this forms fog, and at higher levels, it forms clouds.

Types of clouds

There are three main groups of clouds. The names of
high-level clouds include the words cirrus or cirro.
Medium-level clouds have names starting with alto.
Low-level clouds have various names. The words
nimbus or nimbo indicate rain-bearing clouds.
Great sheets of clouds have names that include
stratus or strato, meaning layer. Names for clouds
that look like fluffy heaps include the words cumulus
or cumulo, meaning a pile or heap.

High-level clouds

Clouds above 16,400 feet (5,000 m) form a thin,
feathery, white veil that does not completely
blot out the sun. They are made of ice crystals,
not water droplets. There are three types.

In cirrus clouds, the ice crystals
are drawn into feathery streaks
across the sky. They are also
called mares' tails.

Cumulonimbus

Stratus

Cirrus

Cirrocumulus

Cirrostratus

Altostratus

Altocumulus

Stratocumulus

Cumulus

Cirrostratus clouds are formed by ice crystals at high levels, making a layer of white clouds over large parts of the sky. If the sun shines through, it has a halo. If the ice crystals are gathered into small clouds arranged in rows, they are called cirrocumulus.

Medium-level clouds

These thicker, darker clouds form between 6,600 and 16,400 feet (2,000–5,000 m). Altostratus clouds have a thin layer of water droplets or ice crystals that the sun or moon shines through weakly. They can also blot out the sun or moon.

Altocumulus are small cumulus at medium heights, often arranged in rows. The amount of blue sky between the clouds depends on their size and spacing. This kind of cloud cover may be called a mackerel sky.

Low-level clouds

There are five main types of clouds with bases below 6,600 feet (2,000 m). These are usually made entirely of water droplets.

Cumulus are thick clouds with flat bases and clearly outlined billows above. Small clouds with a lot of clear sky between them are fair-weather cumulus. Larger clouds are called towering cumulus and may bring rain.

Stratus is a simple layer of gray clouds with a base between ground level and about 6,600 feet (2,000 m). It may be many hundreds of feet thick but has no clear shape. Stratus clouds may bring drizzle or rain.

Stratocumulus consists of a large number of cumulus clouds with the same base level. The upper parts of the clouds are blurred. Individual clouds may appear in bands, between which the sun may shine.

Nimbostratus can be part of a continuous cloud layer from a few yards above ground to high-level clouds. These clouds produce rain in temperate climates. You can distinguish them from ordinary stratus by the small masses of broken clouds, called scuds, beneath the solid base.

Cumulus clouds can tower to the top of the troposphere. Here, the upward air currents weaken, and strong winds blow across the top of the cloud, carrying the ice crystals horizontally. This creates an anvil shape at the top of the cloud. This is a thunder cloud and can produce very heavy rain, hail, or snow, as well as thunder and lightning.

Nimbostratus

Rain

There could be no life without water. Farmers use water for growing crops and keeping livestock, and every human being needs water for drinking, cooking, and sanitation. Industry also uses vast quantities of water. All of this water comes ultimately from rain or other forms of precipitation.

How much rain?

Rainfall amounts vary enormously from region to region. Mawsynram, in the Meghalaya state of India, receives a record-breaking total of 40 feet (12 m) per year, while at the other end of the scale, less than 0.004 inches (0.1 mm) of rain fall in the Atacama Desert in northern Chile.

Condensation and clouds

When moisture-laden air rises, it is heated by the sun and expands. As the air expands, it becomes light and buoyant compared with the air around it. The less dense air rises by convection. As the air rises, it begins to cool, and eventually the water vapor condenses to form clouds. The temperature at which this happens is called the dew point.

The clouds that sweep across the sky are made of billions of tiny water droplets or ice crystals, but they only give up their water when the conditions are right. For clouds to give up their moisture, they must rise in the atmosphere and be cooled still further. This can happen in different ways, and each way produces a different type of rainfall.

Approaching storm clouds over Mahe Island in the Seychelles. In tropical areas, such storms of heavy convectional rain may occur almost every day during the late afternoon in the rainy season.

CAN WE MAKE IT RAIN?

Scientists discovered that silver iodide crystals grow when they collide with supercooled water droplets, in a similar way to ice crystals. They have tried to make rain fall where there is a shortage of water by flying over a cloud and "seeding" it with ice crystals or chemicals such as dry ice (solid carbon dioxide). But they have not always succeeded.

Convectional rain

Rain in tropical regions is called convectional rain. Here, high temperatures evaporate a lot of moisture from the land. The land heated by the hot sun warms the air above it, and the warm air rises. The strong upward air currents make the air cool, and billowing cumulus clouds start to form. The clouds grow quickly to become towering cumulonimbus, made up of millions of tiny water droplets. As the warm air rises rapidly, the tiny water droplets collide and fuse into larger drops. Finally, they become large enough to fall through the rising air as rain. The average diameter of a water droplet in a cloud is 0.0008 inches (0.02 mm). The diameter of a raindrop is 0.08 inches (2 mm)—100 times larger.

Some raindrops never reach the ground. They evaporate in the warm air beneath the cloud. This is why the bottom of some clouds are dark and ragged, although no rain falls from them. In some regions near the equator, especially near lakes, heavy showers of convectional rain fall every afternoon. The showers usually last only a short time.

Rising air forms clouds, rain, or snow

Sheltered, or leeward, slopes in rain shadow

Warm air carries water vapor above the clouds

Warm, dry air

HOW A MOUNTAIN RANGE CAUSES RELIEF RAINFALL

Relief rainfall

Relief rainfall occurs where warm winds carrying water vapor evaporated from the ocean meet a mountain range. The winds rise, the air cools, and clouds form. These grow and cool as they rise, until they release rain or snow on the windward slopes of the mountains. On the far, or leeward, side, the winds blow downhill. They become warmer as they drop and evaporate moisture from the land. The leeward sides of mountains are often arid, or in a rain shadow.

This can have a dramatic effect on rainfall. The Andes Mountains separate southern Chile from Patagonia. Southern Chile is deluged by more than 100 inches (250 cm) of rain a year, whereas Patagonia often receives less than 8 inches (20 cm). The Great Basin Desert in Nevada has been formed as a result of a prolonged rain shadow effect. It is sheltered by the Sierra and Cascade ranges to the west and the Rocky Mountains in the east.

RAIN OR DRIZZLE?

The difference between rain and drizzle is in the size of the raindrop, rather than how hard it is falling. Water drops with a diameter greater than 0.02 inches (0.5 mm) are classified as rain, whereas smaller drops are described as drizzle.

Air masses and fronts

The weather depends on where the air has come from, its temperature, and whether there are clouds. Much of the weather in Britain and western Europe is caused by air masses from the Atlantic Ocean. One air mass can displace another. The boundaries between them are called fronts. The leading edge of a cold air mass is a cold front, and of a warm air mass, a warm front. Where one air mass is moved out of the way by another, the weather changes along the boundary, or front.

Depressions

Depressions, or lows, are areas where the air pressure at Earth's surface is low. They consist of light, warm, rising air. Depressions bring rain, storms, and changing temperatures. Fresh masses of cold and warm air are constantly produced at the poles and the tropics, but the two do not mix easily. Depressions form along the polar front, where warm air from the tropics meets cold air from the poles. A wave develops along the boundary, which forms a V-shape in which a wedge of warm air is trapped in the cool air. The warm air then rises because it is less dense, creating a low pressure area.

A CROSS SECTION THROUGH A DEPRESSION

Cold front

Cold air

Warm sector

Warm front

Cold air

Heavy rain

Prolonged rain

Winds blow into areas of low pressure from places with higher pressure. They are deflected by Earth's rotation, turning counter-clockwise in the northern hemisphere and clockwise in the southern hemisphere. From a satellite, a depression appears as a mass of air that swirls like a stirred cup of tea. As the winds turn around it, the lighter warm air rises up and over the denser cold air. The front of the wedge of warm air is a warm front. There is a sequence of clouds, rain or snow, and temperature change as a warm front crosses an area. The dense cold air forces itself under the warm air from behind, forming a cold front with lower temperatures, heavy rain, and storms.

A satellite photograph of a swirl of clouds, which marks a depression over the North Atlantic. Parts of Britain and continental Europe are visible at the bottom right. Sometimes such depressions in the middle latitudes bring destructive gales and storms, especially in winter.

Occlusions

The wedge of warm air is gradually pushed higher and higher until it no longer touches the ground. Cold fronts move faster than warm fronts, and sometimes a cold front catches up with a warm front, and the two merge. These are known as occluded fronts, or occlusions. Here the weather is unsettled, with clouds, rain, and wind lasting for some time.

The path of a depression

You can usually tell when a depression is coming by the clouds that form. First to appear are cirrus clouds, then altocumulus, followed by stratus clouds. Last of all, at the cold front, come cumulonimbus, the big anvil-shaped rain clouds.

A depression moves along a path or track. Most travel northeasterly in the northern hemisphere and southeasterly in the southern. Weather forecasters try to predict these paths. Depressions last only a day or two but often travel in families of three or four, with ridges of high pressure that bring short, sunny intervals between them.

Jet streams

About six to nine miles (10–15 km) above Earth, in the troposphere, are narrow, winding bands of very strong winds called jet streams, caused by the large differences in temperature between adjacent air masses along the polar front. The greater the difference in temperature, the stronger the jet stream; they can move at speeds of 300 miles (480 km) per hour.

Jet streams circle Earth from west to east in both hemispheres. Where a jet stream bends away from the pole, it makes a trough where depressions form. Each jet stream steers the frontal depressions beneath it across the Atlantic and Pacific Oceans. Jet streams affect air travel. Over the Atlantic, they can slow down flights from Europe to North America or speed up flights in the opposite direction.

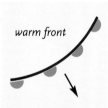

warm front

FRONTS

On a weather map, a warm front is shown by a line with red semicircles pointing in the direction of travel. A cold front is shown as a line with blue triangles pointing in the direction in which the front is going.

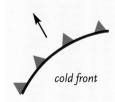

cold front

Thunderstorms

Thunderstorms sometimes occur on hot days when moist air close to the ground is heated and rises quickly. These rapidly rising air currents lead to the formation of towering cumulonimbus clouds with anvil-shaped tops. They may be only a mile (1.6 km) across and yet tower 12 miles (20 km) or so into the sky.

Inside a thundercloud, strong upward and downward air currents sweep ice crystals, ice pellets, and water droplets past and into each other. These movements create static electricity, which builds up in the cloud. Positive electric charges collect toward the top of the cloud, and negative charges collect in the lower parts. The opposing electrical charges are strongly attracted to each other. Eventually, the insulating layer of air between the charges cannot keep them apart, and a massive spark—lightning—is released as the charges neutralize each other.

The lightning discharge can be within a cloud, between clouds, or between a cloud and the air. Only one in four lightning flashes travels from a cloud to the ground. Lightning is attracted to higher parts of Earth's surface, which is why there are lightning conductors on high buildings and why it is dangerous to shelter under a tree in a thunderstorm. One of the safest places is inside a car, as the tires provide insulation.

Sheet lightning within a cloud and cloud to ground lightning, two of the main types of lightning, are visible in this storm over southeast Arizona. Usually only about one in four lightning bolts reaches the ground.

Hailstorms are most common in the middle latitudes, but large hailstones are unusual. Hail formation requires the strong updrafts associated with spring and summer storms.

Thunder and lightning

A lightning flash is hotter than 40,000 °F (22,000 °C). It superheats the air around it, making it expand at an incredible speed and then contract equally rapidly. This creates the sound waves we hear as thunder. Light travels faster than sound, so we see the lightning flash before we hear the thunder. The closer together they are, the nearer the storm. Light travels at 185,000 miles (299,000 km) per second, whereas it takes sound three seconds to travel 0.62 mile (1 km).

What is hail?

Thunderclouds are so tall that their upper levels are well below the freezing point. A raindrop on a strong rising current may be swept up so high that it freezes, only to fall again as the current weakens. At lower levels, the frozen raindrop may collect more water, which freezes on the next upward thrust. This process can be repeated many times. Eventually, spherical pellets of ice called hail fall to the ground.

Most are the size of peas, but in parts of America and other middle latitudes, hailstones the size of golf or even tennis balls can fall. Here, hailstones with 25 layers of ice have been recorded. At this size, they can wreak enormous damage.

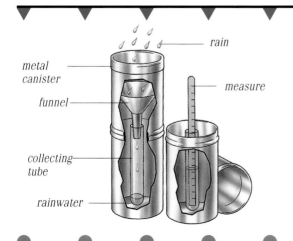

rain

metal canister

funnel

measure

collecting tube

rainwater

MEASURING RAINFALL

Rain and all other forms of precipitation are collected in a rain gauge. It consists of a metal funnel that fits into the top of a cylindrical metal canister. Rain, frost, snow, and hail are collected in the funnel and slide down into the small collecting tube. Every morning at 9 A.M., the collecting tube is lifted out carefully. Any snow, frost, or hail is melted, and the water is then poured into a measuring cylinder.

Snow and ice

A landscape covered with a thick layer of fresh snow is a beautiful sight. Snow is common during the winter months in Europe, northern North America, and southern South America. Many mountaintops have a covering of snow, even near the equator.

Ice crystals

Snowflakes are formed from tiny ice crystals in a cloud. They are created when water vapor freezes around minute solid particles in the middle and upper levels of the atmosphere, where temperatures are well below the freezing point. Individual crystals join to make delicate hexagonal star shapes. They grow into triangles, columns, or needles. The shape depends on the temperature and humidity of the air.

Melting snow

Snow falling from a cloud often melts on its way down and reaches the ground as rain. Snow may partially melt, or a mixture of snow and rain can fall together as sleet when the temperature at ground level is just above freezing. As the falling snow melts, it takes heat from the surrounding air, lowering its temperature. This increases the chance that later falls of snow will reach the ground. The ideal condition for snow is a temperature near or just below the freezing point, rather than an extremely cold temperature. The warmer the snow, the more moisture it holds and the bigger the snowflakes will be. Temperatures close to the freezing point allow the snowflakes to melt, freeze again, and join into larger flakes.

AMAZING SNOWFLAKES

German astronomer Johannes Kepler was the first to describe snowflakes accurately. In 1611, he discovered that nearly all ice crystals are six-sided and that no two are exactly alike.
An American farmer, Wilson Bentley (1865–1931), caught snowflakes on a black velvet-covered tray. He teased apart the individual ice crystals, smoothed them out with a feather, and photographed each one magnified.

Types of snow

Heavy snowfalls and strong winds cause drifting, which can block country roads.

Snowflakes formed in temperatures near the freezing point are large and wet and tend to stick to surfaces. They are perfect for making snowballs! When air temperatures are well below freezing, snowflakes are small and powdery and ideal for skiing. Once snow has settled it may melt, and freeze again, becoming harder and slippery to walk or drive on. The wind may blow snow into drifts that can block roads and railways in exposed areas.

Wind-blown snow

Blizzards are snowstorms with strong winds, which can damage telephone and power lines, leaving people without heat and light. The wind chill in a blizzard can be very dangerous for people outdoors. When blizzards hit Colorado in October 1997, the storms dropped 71.4 inches (183 cm) of snow in two days and killed 11 people. In Denver, the state capital, 1,000 vehicles were abandoned.

Avalanches

A buildup of snow in mountain areas can lead to an avalanche. The most common kind of avalanche begins when an unstable mass of snow breaks away from a slope. As the snow gains speed, it collects more snow, soil, and rock. The whole mass rushes downhill at speeds that can reach 186 miles (300 km) per hour, destroying everything in its path.

An avalanche on Shispar Peak in Pakistan caused by fresh powdery snow breaking loose from older snow beneath.

Ice storms

Winter storms can also bring ice. Ice storms are formed when rain that has fallen through warmer air meets a layer of very cold air near the ground. The rain does not have time to change to sleet. Instead, it turns to ice when it touches any solid object.

In January 1998, a severe ice storm lasting five days raged over eastern Canada and the northeastern U.S. In Maine alone, more than 220,000 people lost power. The ice destroyed 2,500 power poles and brought down thousands of miles of power lines. Falling trees and icy roads made travel almost impossible. In eastern Canada, the storm brought down 80,000 miles (129,000 km) of power lines and 1,000 power poles, leaving three million people without power.

Black ice

Black ice is not black. It is glazed or clear ice that forms when rain or drizzle falls on a surface with a temperature below the freezing point. It is difficult to see because it is clear, and the road shows through.

Colorful skies

8

Our skies are an ever-changing display of colors. They include the rich blues of a cloud-free day, the reds, pinks, and golds of sunrise and sunset, and, occasionally, greens and purples. Many of these colors are created as a reaction between sunlight and water and dust in the atmosphere.

When the sun is low in the sky, the path of its rays through the atmosphere is longer, and yellow, orange, and red colors are scattered near the ground.

Color and light

Although sunlight looks white, it is really made up of different wavelengths of light that have different colors. The colors are those seen in a rainbow—red, orange, yellow, green, blue, indigo, and violet. Each color travels at a different wavelength: red and orange have the longest wavelengths, while indigo and blue have the shortest.

As sunlight travels through the atmosphere, the light waves are scattered in different directions by dust, pollutants, and the gas molecules that make up the air. The blue in sunlight is the most scattered and creates the blue sky we see on sunny days. We see the deepest blues when the air is dry, cold, and clean. Water droplets and dust particles increase the scattering so that there are more green and yellow rays, which turn the sky a paler blue.

Sunrise, sunset, and twilight

As the sun rises or sets, its light has to travel farther through the atmosphere, and through more clouds and dust, to reach our eyes. Much of the blue light is lost, and more colors from the red and orange wavelengths are scattered, which creates the colors we see at the beginning or end of the day. Twilight is also the result of the scattering of light. As night approaches, we are not plunged into darkness because of the dust and other impurities in the atmosphere. These particles scatter light from the sky and reflect it into Earth's shadow, causing the soft rays of twilight after the sun has set.

RED SKIES

During the mid-1880s, people in many parts of the world noticed that the sunsets were unusually red. They were caused by the greatest volcanic eruption in modern times—of Krakatoa in Indonesia in 1883. The gigantic explosion shot smoke and dust more than 30 miles (50 km) into the atmosphere, where it colored the sunsets.

White clouds

Clouds are white because of the scattering of light by the water droplets from which they are made. In clouds, the colors of the rainbow recombine to produce white light. If light does not pass through the clouds to the ground, or if another cloud casts a shadow, the clouds may appear gray or even black.

How rainbows form

When white light passes through a clear substance, such as glass or water, it is bent at a slight angle, or refracted. Colors of different wavelengths are refracted at slightly different angles, so the process causes the colors of white light to separate into bands called a spectrum. You sometimes see this array of colors when sunlight shines through a glass of water. You can see it even better if you shine white light through a triangular piece of glass called a prism.

A rainbow is a spectrum in the sky. The colors are brightest at the foot because the largest raindrops are there.

A rainbow is created when raindrops refract sunlight. The raindrops act like minute prisms, and each color emerges from a raindrop at a slightly different angle. The same color emerges at the same angle from every one of the millions of raindrops in the cloud, so from the ground we see bands of colors—a spectrum in the sky.

The rainbow is part of a circle, but we usually see only the part above the horizon. You might see the full circle if you looked down on a rainbow from an aircraft. In a double rainbow, the main rainbow has red at the top. The second, fainter rainbow has the colors in reverse order.

Halos and coronas

A halo is the name for the luminous discs that sometimes appear around the sun or, less often, the moon. Halos are caused by the slight bending, or refraction, of light as it passes through a thin layer of high-level clouds made up of ice crystals. Similar effects, called coronas, appear when we see the sun or moon through a thin layer of clouds made up of water droplets.

Northern and southern lights

The spectacular display of moving lights and colors created by the auroras are breathtaking. The auroras are called the northern lights, or aurora borealis, in the northern hemisphere, and the southern lights, or aurora australis, in the southern hemisphere. They are most often seen in the polar regions, but you can see them at lower latitudes from time to time.

The auroras are created when the sun emits fast-moving, electrically charged particles, known as the solar wind. Most of the world, aside from the polar regions, is protected from these particles by Earth's magnetic field. In the unprotected polar regions, the charged particles collide with the air molecules in Earth's atmosphere. They give out energy in the form of red, green, and white lights. These ascend in flickering sheets and streaks, roughly in the shape of a fan. The interaction between the solar wind and the air takes place between 95 and 310 miles (150–500 km) above Earth's surface.

Auroras, or northern and southern lights, are shimmering curtains of light caused when bursts of electrically charged particles from the sun enter Earth's atmosphere. This display of the northern lights was in the sky over northern Norway.

Weather recording and forecasting

9

To make a weather forecast, meteorologists piece together information from thousands of weather stations and other sources across the world. When this information is compiled, they can begin to predict what the weather will be like. Nowadays, electronic instruments record much of the weather information automatically.

Collecting information

Temperature, pressure, and rainfall figures are needed to forecast the weather, as well as wind speed and direction, humidity, visibility, and the type, amount, and height of the clouds. This information is collected day and night by thousands of people on land and at sea, and by automatic weather recording devices. Some ships carry equipment to record the weather conditions, and weather buoys (either moored or drifting freely and powered by the sun's energy) provide a continuous stream of information.

A weather station on top of an Austrian mountain. The white Stevenson screen protects the instruments from sunlight and radiation.

Weather stations

The simplest land-based weather station is a Stevenson screen. This wooden box on legs protects the instruments inside from sunlight and radiation from the ground. Air enters through the sides. Observers visit daily to copy down the information recorded. Today, most weather information is collected by small, automatic stations on land around the world. They may be powered by the sun and relay readings to forecasting centers by satellites.

Weather balloons

Weather forecasters also need to know the state of the atmosphere above Earth's surface. One of the best ways of collecting this information is with a radiosonde. This is a package of instruments carried skyward by a helium-filled balloon.

A scientist launching a radiosonde balloon at the Halley Research Station in Antarctica.

Radiosonde balloons are released several times a day from weather stations in many parts of the world. They are tracked by radar, which gives wind speed and direction, and contain a small radio transmitter that sends back details of the atmospheric pressure, temperature, and humidity. At 12.4 miles (20 km), they burst, and the package parachutes to Earth.

Aircraft and satellites

Many civil aircraft radio back weather information on intercontinental journeys. Meteorological satellites orbit Earth, tracking the movements of hurricanes and collecting information in the upper atmosphere. Remote sensors on some measure sea temperatures, wave height, and even the thickness of sea-ice. Others carry radar that can show moving rain or snow.

There are two kinds of weather satellites. Geostationary satellites show the same part of Earth's surface all the time. They remain above the same point on Earth's surface, orbiting at the same speed. Others orbit Earth roughly from pole to pole. During a three-day orbit, they send back a stream of pictures. Today, land-based radar helps meteorologists monitor rain, snow and storms over an area.

Weather maps

Meteorologists publish their findings on a weather map called a synoptic chart, which is marked with symbols. This map shows isobars—lines joining places with the same atmospheric pressure. Barometer readings are marked in millibars or inches (1,000 mb = 29.54 inches). Anticyclones and depressions are marked "high" (H) and "low" (L) respectively, while symbols show the wind speed and direction. Bold lines mark warm and cold fronts, and half circles and arrows on them show the direction in which they are moving.

MAKING A FORECAST

To make forecasts, meteorologists gather all of the available information and feed it into a computer that can perform millions of calculations a second. They produce weather maps using mathematical models based on their knowledge of what creates the weather. At present, even the most powerful computer cannot predict the weather with reasonable accuracy more than about five days in advance.

A synoptic chart, which uses symbols to give a synopsis, or summary, of the weather over the U.S. at a particular time.

Changing weather patterns

10

Earth's climate has changed many times since Earth was formed about 4,600 million years ago. Sometimes, Earth has been much hotter than it is now; at other times, much land has been covered by ice and snow during Ice Ages.

Coral fossils in this limestone found in Scotland show that when the rock was formed, the sediments settled in warm, shallow, tropical seas. This shows that the British Isles were once much closer to the equator.

Information from rocks

By studying layers of rocks, geologists can tell what the climate was like when they were formed. Sandstone and limestone are common rocks in Britain and North America. We know that sandstone was formed millions of years ago in ancient deserts, while limestone is largely composed of ancient corals and was formed in warm, shallow, tropical seas.

The last Ice Age

Tens of thousands of years ago, early man lived in the grip of the last of the Ice Ages, which peaked about 18,000 years ago. Temperatures were several degrees lower than today, and vast glaciers and ice sheets covered large parts of Europe, Scandinavia, and North America. In the southern hemisphere, much of Argentina, New Zealand, and parts of Australia and South Africa were also covered—about a third of Earth's surface altogether. Stone Age paintings and engravings in caves in the Sahara Desert show that it was grassland during the last Ice Age and that lions, giraffes, elephants, and hippopotamuses lived there. Sea levels were lower, and people could walk from mainland Europe to what is now the British Isles, or from Russia to the present-day U.S.

This antelope carved by Stone Age people on the wall of a cave in the Sahara Desert in Algeria suggests that the area was once grassland.

The end of the Ice Age

The last Ice Age started to end about 12,000 years ago. Earth began to warm, and the ice began to melt. As sea levels rose, early people became more isolated from each other. By about 7,000 years ago, the coastlines of the continents had begun to take on their present shape.

We now live in a warm period, but climatologists and historians have discovered that since the end of the last Ice Age there have been periods when it was warmer or cooler than today.

Modern changes to climate

Scientists have many theories to explain these changes. Recent studies show that major volcanic eruptions can cause cold weather. The volcanic dust blocks out sunlight and cools Earth. Some scientists think that gradual changes in Earth's orbit around the sun or the tilt of its axis may have caused the climatic changes. These changes may have meant that the northern hemisphere received less of the sun's heat than before and became colder.

Today, our weather is changing because of human activities. Weather changes include the formation of acid rain and photochemical smog, the growing hole in the ozone layer, and global warming. These all result from our continued pollution of the atmosphere by wasteful industrial processes and fuel-inefficient methods of transportation, from the Industrial Revolution onward.

Acid rain

Acid rain describes the acidity of rain and other forms of precipitation, including hail, sleet, snow, mist, fog, and dew. Rainfall is always slightly acidic because carbon dioxide gas in the atmosphere dissolves in rainwater to form a weak acid called carbonic acid. However, burning

Scientists uncover a woolly mammoth from the ice in northern Russia. Mammoths became extinct 10,000 to 12,000 years ago. Microorganisms and pollen grains preserved in the body tell us about the climate at that time.

fossil fuels, such as coal, oil, and natural gas, produces waste gases, including sulphur dioxide and oxides of nitrogen. Combined with moisture in the atmosphere, these produce sulphuric and nitric acids and make the rain even more acidic.

Acid rain damages freshwater fisheries, lakes, streams, groundwater, forests, crops, buildings, statues, and human health. It is not a local problem. Once the acid gases reach the atmosphere, pollution may be carried thousands of miles. Acid rain produced by one country can damage the environment of another. The areas most at risk are in Europe and North America, but many parts of the world are threatened.

Acid rain and other pollutants are killing these conifers on a mountainside in Switzerland.

A police officer wears a mask as protection against acid fumes while he directs traffic in southeast Asia.

The effects of smog

When there is fog in cities and industrial areas, particles of solid matter, especially from smoke, are trapped in the atmosphere. The resulting mixture of smoke and fog is known as smog. In persistent smog, so much soot may accumulate in the fog that it is dangerous to breathe it. In December 1952, smog covered London, and about 4,000 people were killed by the polluted air. Smog is rare today because smokeless zones have been created, and smoke from factories is better controlled.

A growing problem is the smog produced by vehicle exhausts. In some weather conditions, the exhaust gases emitted by vehicles cannot escape into the upper atmosphere. They produce a severe form of air pollution. Cities such as Los Angeles and Mexico City are surrounded by hills. Calm weather traps vehicle fumes here, and sunlight changes them into damaging ozone and choking smog. This type of pollution is called photochemical smog. In recent years, areas of India and Southeast Asia have been affected by a brownish-colored haze caused by fumes from traffic, power stations, factories, and the smoke from fires used to clear forest areas. Air pollution of this kind leads to a huge increase in people with breathing problems such as asthma, bronchitis, and lung infections.

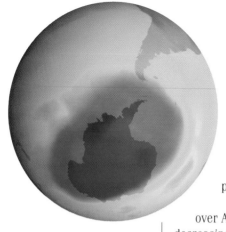

The ozone layer

Ozone is a form of oxygen in very small amounts in the atmosphere. The highest concentrations are in the stratosphere, about 12.4 to 15.5 miles (20–25 km) above Earth's surface. Ozone has a number of roles. Most importantly, it shields Earth's surface against ultraviolet radiation from the sun, which would otherwise harm people, plants, and animals.

Over the last 30 years, scientists measuring ozone levels over Antarctica and elsewhere have noticed that they are decreasing and that a hole is forming in the ozone layer. They believe the cause is a group of chemicals known as chlorofluorocarbons (CFCs). These were once widely used in aerosols, refrigeration and air-conditioning units, dry cleaning, and the plastic foam used to make hamburger cartons. CFCs have now been banned in many countries, but scientists think it will take 50 years for the ozone layer to repair itself.

The Antarctic ozone hole reaches a maximum each spring. The thinnest part of the ozone layer is shown in dark blue.

Tropical rain forest is cleared by fire on the island of Borneo, Malaysia.

GREENHOUSE GASES

There are more than 30 other greenhouse gases, including nitrous oxide, given out by fertilizers, exhausts, and coal-fired power stations. This gas traps 270 times more heat than the same amount of carbon dioxide. Another greenhouse gas is methane, produced by microbes in swamps and by animal manure. It is also released when fossil fuels are burned and domestic waste is buried where it can rot. Other greenhouse gases include CFCs and ozone.

Global warming and the greenhouse effect

More and more scientists have produced evidence that the world's climate is becoming warmer. They believe this is due largely to pollution of the atmosphere.

Carbon dioxide is one of the gases that makes up the air we breathe. Over the last 100 years, the amount in the atmosphere has increased, mainly because of the burning of fossil fuels and the clearance of forests by burning. Heat from the sun is absorbed by Earth's surface. Most of this heat is then radiated away from Earth, and some escapes back into space. Carbon dioxide and some other gases allow the sun's energy to pass through to Earth, but they trap the heat coming back from the surface of Earth. They act in the same way as the glass in a greenhouse, which retains warmth. Earth needs this greenhouse, effect. If gases such as carbon dioxide did not absorb some of the heat radiating from Earth, the world would be colder. The oceans would freeze and the average temperature would be 0 °F (-18 °C).

Until recently, the world's natural levels of carbon dioxide had kept Earth at a comfortable average temperature of 59 °F (15 °C). However, since the start of the Industrial Revolution, people have been changing the composition of the atmosphere. We are building up a chemical blanket of carbon dioxide and other gases that trap more of the heat that used to escape. The result is an increase in temperature.

The effects of global warming

The average world temperature has risen by more than 1 °F (0.5 °C) in the last 150 years. Scientists estimate that it could rise by 5.4 °F (3 °C) by 2050 and 10.5 °F (5.8 °C) by the end of the century. The last Ice Age was ended by a rise in temperature of only 5 to 7 °F (3–4 °C).

Most climatologists believe that the world's weather will continue to become more extreme, with more storms, hurricanes, and tornadoes. Water will be scarcer in some places, and sea levels will rise as polar ice melts. Islands and low-lying cities will be flooded. Diseases such as malaria and cholera, and deaths from heat stroke and skin cancer, will increase. Some crops will not grow where they are grown now. Crop yields will drop in some regions. Some plants and animals that cannot adapt will become extinct. You can read more about these changes in *Changing Climates*, another book in this series. Meanwhile, everyone can do their part to help reduce the effects of climate change.

Wind turbines create electricity without polluting the atmosphere.

Glossary

acid rain   Rain that is more acidic than usual because of the polluting gases from power stations and vehicle exhausts that are dissolved in it.

advection fog   Fog formed when warm, moist air passes over a cooler surface.

air pressure   The force of the air pressing down on Earth's surface.

anemometer   An instrument for measuring wind speed.

anticyclone   A large area of high pressure (sometimes called a high) from which all winds blow outward.

atmosphere   The blanket of gases around a planet, held there by the pull of the planet's gravity.

aurora   Bands of colored lights that appear in the sky. In the northern hemisphere, they are called the northern lights, or the aurora borealis; in the southern hemisphere, they are called the southern lights, or aurora australis.

avalanche   A rapid movement of snow, sometimes combined with ice and rock material, down a steep slope.

barometer   An instrument for measuring air pressure.

blizzard   Severe weather conditions combining heavy snow, strong winds, low temperatures, and poor visibility.

climate   The average weather in a place over a long period of time.

clouds   Masses of water droplets or ice particles floating in the atmosphere. There are 10 types of clouds, with three basic groups: stratus, cumulus, and cirrus.

condensation   The process by which a vapor or gas changes into a liquid as it cools.

Coriolis effect   The way that the direction of the wind is turned by the spin of Earth—to the right in the northern hemisphere and to the left in the southern hemisphere. The Coriolis force is strongest at the poles and weakens toward the equator, where it disappears altogether.

current   A body of air or water moving in a definite direction.

cyclone   (see hurricane)

depression   An area of low pressure, sometimes called a low, which brings unsettled weather. It may also be called a cyclone.

dew point   The temperature at which water vapor in the air will condense.

evaporation   The process by which a liquid is changed into a vapor or gas when it is heated.

fossil fuel   A fuel produced from the fossil remains of plants or animals: coal, peat, oil, or natural gas.

front   The boundary between two masses of air at different temperatures. Rain often occurs along a front.

global warming   The warming of Earth's atmosphere as a result of air pollution.

greenhouse effect   The warming of Earth caused by certain gases in the atmosphere, called greenhouse gases. These allow the sun's rays to reach Earth's surface but trap heat given off by the ground.

humidity   The amount of water vapor in the air.

hurricane   A violent tropical storm in the Caribbean and North Atlantic with winds blowing at 73 miles (118 km) per hour or more around a low pressure center. It is known as a typhoon in the northwestern Pacific and a cyclone in the Indian Ocean.

Ice Age   One of several periods in Earth's history when huge glaciers and ice sheets covered large parts of the land surface.

ice storm A storm in which falling rain freezes as soon as it touches any object that is below the freezing point.

jet stream A narrow band of very strong winds in the upper levels of the troposphere.

meteorology The study of how the atmosphere creates the weather and climate.

monsoon A wind that blows from different directions at different times of the year, causing wet and dry seasons, particularly in southern Asia, northern Australia, and western Africa.

occlusion The condition of the atmosphere when an advancing cold front overtakes a warm front, raising the warm sector of the depression and cutting it off from Earth's surface.

ozone layer A layer of ozone gas (a form of oxygen) in Earth's atmosphere, which absorbs 90 percent of the harmful ultraviolet rays from the sun.

polar front The boundary (or front) between warm tropical air and cold polar air in the middle latitudes north and south of the equator. Frontal depressions form and travel along it.

precipitation Any form of water (solid or liquid) that

falls from the atmosphere and reaches the ground.

prevailing wind The main direction from which the wind blows in particular places.

radiation fog Fog that forms at night in low-lying areas when the air is moist, the sky is clear, and there is little wind. The ground cools quickly, cooling the air above.

rain shadow An area of decreased rainfall on the lee, or sheltered, side of a hill or mountain.

relative humidity The ratio between the actual amount of water vapor in the air and the maximum amount it can hold at a given temperature.

relief rainfall Rainfall resulting from hills and mountains causing clouds to rise and cool.

snow line The lowest level on a mountain above which snow never disappears.

spectrum Bands of colors like those seen in a rainbow, formed by splitting white light into its constituent colors.

stratosphere The layer of the atmosphere that lies above the troposphere.

synoptic chart A weather chart that provides detailed information about weather conditions at a particular

time over a large area.

timberline The highest point at which trees grow on a mountain.

tornado An intense, rotating column of air, shaped like a funnel or rope, that extends down from the base of a cloud to the ground.

trade wind Steady winds in the tropics blowing from the northeast in the northern hemisphere and from the southeast in the southern hemisphere.

troposphere The layer of the atmosphere that is closest to Earth. This is where our weather occurs.

ultraviolet rays Invisible rays given off by the sun and other very hot objects. Ultraviolet rays can burn the skin and cause skin cancer.

vacuum A completely empty space without air in it.

water cycle The continuous circulation of water from Earth's surface to the atmosphere, involving evaporation, condensation, and precipitation.

waterspout A rotating column of air that extends downward from the base of a cloud to touch a water surface. It is usually less violent than a tornado.

water vapor Water in the form of an invisible gas.

Index